ANGEL BELLS

By
Judith Christian-Moon

Stories and Poetry
In the
Journey of Grief

Copyright © 2016 by Judith Christian-Moon

Angel Bells
by Judith Christian-Moon

Printed in the United States of America.

ISBN 9781498486323

All rights reserved solely by the author. The author guarantees all contents are original and do not infringe upon the legal rights of any other person or work. No part of this book may be reproduced in any form without the permission of the author. The views expressed in this book are not necessarily those of the publisher.

Unless otherwise indicated, Scripture quotations taken from the King James Version (KJV)–*public domain*.

Scripture quotations taken from the New King James Version (NKJV). Copyright © 1982 by Thomas Nelson, Inc. Used by permission. All rights reserved.

Scripture quotations taken from the Holy Bible, New International Version (NIV). Copyright © 1973, 1978, 1984, 2011 by Biblica, Inc.™ Used by permission. All rights reserved.

www.xulonpress.com

Table of contents

Introduction vii
The Journey 9
Death and the Survivor... 70
About the Author.. 73

Introduction

My journey, through each death of my two wonderful husbands, was at a much different level than my journey through grief over the death of my father several years before.

Perhaps the difference was that my dear first husband walked that journey with me during my dad's illness with cancer and his death that year on Good Friday. Perhaps it was different because of the shock of my first husband's death, or the length of time to prepare…he went running one Sunday morning and didn't come home—his heart attack was fatal.

One would think that losing a beloved spouse in death would prepare one for the passing of a second spouse—especially since the discovery of the presence of Alzheimer's Disease in that dear one should cause one to be prepared for a long uncertain journey.

No, my friend, one is never prepared for the sense of loss one feels after the death of a loved one.

I have found that personal belief in God is a great sustaining power and that the HOPE of being reunited with our loved one, at the feet of Jesus, is quite enabling, as one tries to get on with the reality of living.

I pray that this book brings you some insight into the journey, Even some comfort.

My prayer for you, my friend, is that as you read these words and poems, your own journey will be eased. The words seemed to come to me as Angel Bells that brought great comfort in my journey. I pray that you will find strength and comfort, as you get on with the reality of living every day.

ANGEL BELLS

The poem comes together as words do their part,
Pealing like Angel bells in my heart.
They bring phrases that give relief
And aid in the healing of very deep grief.

Angel bells pealing loud and long,
Bring to my heart a brand new song.
A song to sing as healing takes place,
A song to thank God for mercy and grace.

A song of thanksgiving for days of yore,
A song of praise that there will be more.
A song of joy for hope in tomorrow,
A song to find strength, even in sorrow.

Angel bells do their job very well.
Angel bells have a message to tell.
Angel bells peal in hearts full of grief.
Angel bells pealing the gift of relief.

Grief Work

Time does not heal grief.
It takes work and effort.
It's work to cry daily, hourly,
    to talk about him,
    to answer cards and letters,
    to go out to eat,
    to get the car serviced,
    to clean out his tool chest,
    to rearrange his camera closet,
    to use our everyday dishes,
    to cook his favorite food,
    to be alone.

Real Victory

Loved ones around me in the hospital,
I still felt alone, the pain was too real.
They spoke in words, hushed and low.
They stayed real close so I would know,
They, too, felt pain over our loss.
We thanked God for the love of the Cross.

Those outstretched arms, offering love to all,
Who come to Him and, in repentance, fall
At His feet in total submission,
Asking for mercy and to be forgiven.
Mercy is given with forgiveness and love,
As also are grace and peace from above.

So, today, we feel comfort to some degree
That this loved one is now in eternity.
Our pain is eased, though real it be,
For we know that he, one day, we'll see.
We rejoice in the truth that every Christian knows.
After the pain of death, Our Lord arose.
That's …….real victory.

FROM HERE TO ETERNITY

Death seems so final, but it's not the end.
What do we really know, dear friend?
It really does matter what you do think,
For death is a step-quick as a blink.
It's a step in time and space,
That takes us to that judgment place.
In that blink, time is not measured,
And we are exposed for what we have treasured.
After death, at judgment day, we will see
Just where we will spend eternity.

Tears of Grief Heal

The death of a loved one means many tears shed,
Triggered by memories like when we were wed.
Tears of self-pity help healing begin
To get over the loss of a very special friend.
Tears of anger, sadness and frustration
Are, to my grief, a balm of medication.
There are memories that bring tears of pride.
These tears allow grief to stem the tide,
Physically and emotionally, tears seem to boss,
And they help to condition me to the loss.

WORDS TO NOT INK

Words are coming and they are going.
I can't ink them and let my emotions be showing.
Why, right now, do I feel like this?
Why have my thoughts taken this twist?

Some prose that shows how my mind is being jerked around right now. I realize that these are not complete sentences, but that is just how I am feeling during these days. I am not complete, nor am I able to focus. Therefore, I share these incomplete thoughts that are meaningful to me.

I don't think cycling would be a source of fun for me, as it was for the two of us…I no longer feel it's a part of my life. I probably should get rid of the motorcycle.

I am the only one I have to answer to, now. The children, grandchildren and friends ask about what my plans are….I'm not ready to put any into words yet.

In a hurry to get home to him (past tense).

Now, what's the hurry? Why speed or drive fast?

So, now I leave early and arrive where I'm going early.

If the event was important enough to me to enter it on my calendar, I'll go. Otherwise, I may just stay home and cry.

Why keep getting the daily paper? I only read the Sunday paper thoroughly, sometimes.

This first year: just doing what's required to do to function.

The second year: beginning to see people and places, and setting goals for outings.

My grief is like radar—it has taught me to search out the pain in people and to share HOPE. To be a source of comfort—to shed tears of empathy.

Death is so final, yet it is but a blink until judgment day and eternity, as a step in time and space.

Evenings and weekends are now empty time; they once were our time together. We enjoyed planning or taking trips for work or vacation.

I grieve for myself—I pity me. I'm alone—he was a part of me and now that part is gone. I'm a "part"—a fragment, a piece of a whole—a remnant. Incomplete.

Most people see me as an independent and strong woman, who can handle almost any task and, perhaps, I gave that impression when I knew I had David to back me up in everything.

I have never lived alone, until David died—I went from my families' home to a roommate at the University, to marriage—-now, ALONE. Alone at fifty-five years of age.

And now alone again, as Loyd progresses into that illness of loss of memory and ability—then really alone again as he dies on another Good Friday. Alone—at age sixty-eight, with pain too deep to speak or even cry—again, it's just me and Jesus.

Besides my Bible, many books have helped me on my journey. Some of these books are:

"God in the Dark" by Luci Shaw
"Widowed" by Joyce Brothers
"The Inheritance" by Joyce Landdorf
"Hands Across the Seasons" by Gloria Gaither

As for my grief journey in Alzheimer's Disease, I found much help and support by being a part of the Alzheimer's Association and support groups. Now, I am glad to be able to facilitate a group with the hope to "be there" for caregivers and loved ones of those with A.D.

Does Grief Work Make Us Self-centered?

So immersed in my own grief work that I neglected to give aid to my children, who each were struggling in their own way through grief; each directing their frustrations in varied ways. My girls were "daddy's girls", and my sons had truly belonged to their dad—I was just mom—there all the time—but dad was special and always said the right thing, and knew what to do. He was their only dad and now, they felt orphaned. They cried, had insomnia and trouble coping with day to day activities for several months. They were left unprotected from death by the death of their dad—now they were the next generation.

Even the caring spouses of my children were affected by his death, because they had each bonded so well with their loved one's dad that he was a part of their lives. They found pain in grief real. All suffered torments of unfinished business between themselves and their dad—father-in-law. The "if onlys" were constantly coming up in their conversations.

The grandchildren suffered the loss of one they had learned to know was really special and now, all of a sudden, he was gone. Their curiosity about death –not totally explained—and, therefore, quite confusing for all their ages. Their grief is complicated by fears that their own parent might die soon.

I'm thankful for my friends, who let me talk about him—-on and on.....

I lost the one to laugh with; to share with; to try out new dishes; to talk to while he was rotating the tires on the car; to compliment me on my hair and clothes, my speech, my poems, my crafts...

I've developed a letter and e-mail relationship with several people who share my love for poetry.

I've taken a year of classes on CPE (clinical pastoral education) to hone my skills in crisis counseling and ministering to families in need.

My circle of widowed friends is increasing, and I find joy in sharing of understanding.

I take time for the hairdresser weekly.

If I feel like crying, I do.

I know death is a part of life, but it took so much from me as a part of my self-identity and purpose for setting goals. I was overwhelmed. Tears do help...emotionally and physically. Tears of self-pity, sadness, frustration, helplessness and anger allowed me to become conditioned to the loss.

When I see a couple irritated with each other, I want to tell them to "make good memories—time's precious...too soon, one of you will be alone".

I cling to the familiar: church, club, dentist, library, restaurant, hairstyle, groceries, car.

I realize that the family no longer revolves around us and our schedules, ie., Thanksgiving, etc. It is a natural evolution...the children are the key generation—building traditions for their families.

Oh, how I wish to concentrate
On things to be done—that just can't wait.
But since I've lost my power to reason,
Some things must be put-off till another season.

THE CEMETERY

As I spend time at the cemetery,
I wonder about what makes me tarry.
I know that he's not really here,
But my being here brings focus clear.

At home, I wait for his return.
While here, I claim the truths I've learned.
Truths that tell me there is hope,
As with questions I now grope.

It is so peaceful and quiet here.
I hear thoughts in my mind so clear.
The air is still, save the birds as they fly,
And an occasional car on the road that runs by.
The flowers in stands to hold them secure
Have been brought by those who've lost someone dear.

Where My Husband Was Laid

The greenery was limp and swayed in the breeze.
The purples now violet with fragrance, but a tease.
The sun had shown strong
And the rains had come long.
The flowers had begun to fade,
At the place where my husband was laid.

And yet in my mind, it was yesterday
When we all stood there and put him away.
When our faces were swollen from crying all night,
And we'd change it all quickly if only we might.
So vital to me was each precious hour,
When together we stood and found real power.

We'll put out new flowers of bright, sunny colors
And know that they'll be replaced by others.
We come to this place-not to find him,
But to honor the memory of one who was kin.
As my husband, he was more than kin to me
And I know in my heart he'll forever be.

Though flowers may wilt and memories may fade,
I'll return to the place where my husband was laid.
I'll write poems and cards for my living friends,
And tell them "I love you" until my life ends.

TWO

The two of us, so much in love,
Began a marriage shaped above.
We didn't know what we NOW know.
Although we'd probable still say, "go",
And "go" we did to build our home.
To build a home that God would own,
A home that grew as the years went past.
A home built on love that was meant to last,
A home He'd begun with just us two,
Now has grown to twenty-two.

TYPICAL

Today is another typical day.
From my house, I'm far away.
I see my lifestyle changing fast.
Sometimes I long for days in the past.

Not that I try to resist progress,
Nor from change do I digress.
But I long for days when I knew
Where to go and what to do.

Maybe soon I'll stabilize,
And in my schedule I'll realize
That what I do and where I go
Are because God has guided so.

I AM A WIDOW

Of what once was a whole, I now am a part.
I feel there's a very large hole in my heart.
As in the charm I wear on my watch,
The watch David got for the retirement he never took.

I still eat, shop and move like I'm real,
But I hope I don't look or act like I feel.
For when David died, a large part of me went,
And I feel no comfort until my knees are bent.

So when I'm alone, a large part of my day
Is spent on my knees, as I kneel to pray.
Even in a crowd, my heart I can bow
To ask Him for comfort, and I need it right now.

After reading John 11:13...

A Christian in Grief

Jesus sees our pain and grief. And it grieves Him to see that. He understands and weeps also. Understanding the HOPE that the death of a Christian has for the survivors is joyful but, still, the pain of personally missing that loved one is quite real.

As I've said earlier—Time doesn't heal grief—hard work does. Remember: this, too, shall pass—not so—just changes. And nothing on earth is forever. Time allows work and experiences with God.

Time doesn't dominate the Christian. Heartaches are limited by time. Problems are limited by time. Diseases are limited by time.

You, my friend, are not limited by time, but have eternity. Therefore you, who are Christian, go ahead and grieve.....grieve by rejoicing.

SINCE HIS DEATH

My life and days are constantly changing,
Even my house I'm rearranging.
Not to change the focus from him,
But trying to adjust to the times I'm in.

Times I find when I must try,
To go beyond wanting to die.
I must make haste and do my best,
Lest I'm not done when I reach my rest.

GUILT IN JOY

I feel I am betraying my love for him,
When I have fun with friends and kin.
For he's not here to have a part
And that brings sadness to my heart.

My heart knows that he's not coming back.
My mind holds tight to our love track.
I'm sure my mind holds on, because
It can't imagine a love as loss.

So I go on, feeling guilt in joy.
Without him, I lack security.
The peace that comes in the reality
Of one close by who really cares
And, for me, does offer prayers.

I miss the support he gave.
Support now stops at the grave.
I miss the words of reality,
Words that were spoken just to me.

I cooked some vegetables today.
They didn't taste just the way
They did when I cooked for him.
When every mouthful brought a grin.

Is it true, as they say,
That recipes cooked any way
Are not well done to bring a grin
Until the love's been added in.

continued

I draw great peace in time of grief,
As I contemplate on my belief.
I thank God that David I knew
And that it was together we grew.

We grew to learn the Father's will
And always tried our place to fill.
Though we were often way off-base,
We never lost sight of the Father's face.

I now take courage in the Lord
And spend much time in His word.
He helps me overcome fear and doubt,
And to know that I am not left out.

HIM (GOD)

As He guides me now in what to do,
I let myself share love with you.
Knowing He prepares the way
Makes it easier to get through the day.

STRENGTH

David was my human strength.
He enhanced my natural senses,
Like how to think, feel and will,
And now his voice to me is still.

The Holy Spirit is my divine strength.
He enhances my spiritual senses,
Like how to pray, study and grow,
And more about my Father's will to know.

Thoughts in my mind are flitting about,
As birds flying over a school of trout,
My mind pulled about by enticing distractions
Is keeping me from more major attractions.

I MISS

I miss so much that way of life,
When I was his "beloved wife".....

Like running my fingers across his back,
When he sat reading, his mind on one track.
Or seeing his smile when our eyes did meet,
Or lying in bed and touching feet.

I miss the friendship we shared together
And how we complimented each other.
He was strong when I was weak.
When I was strong, he needed me.
Life today is so strange—

I miss the things we did together,
Like hiking across a mountain range,
Or cycling along in stormy weather.

I miss our special, secret time—
The hours when he was only mine.
Times when we did each impart
Love that came straight from the heart.

I rearranged the medicine cabinet
To accommodate my make-up habit.
I moved his razor and mug up a shelf.
I don't think I'll use them myself.

I sat in his chair, but felt him not.
His feel and touch, so soon forgot.
And yet he is still as real to me,
As in my mind I allow him to be.

His unseen force pervading my life,
The force of one who called me "wife".
I feel him here, he is so real.
This force I will not let death steal.

SHARED BURDEN

I find some ease as a burden lifted,
And wonder how I was so gifted.
Until I heard a dear friend say,
She'd talked to the Lord about me today.

So I thank You, Lord, for special friends,
Who share with me this great burdens.
I thank You, Lord, for their special love,
A love I know is from above.

COFFEE TIME

His cup now sits on the shelf with mine,
Gathering dust as we bide our time.
They're sitting as useless as I feel.
For me, this time does not seem real.

Today will move on—-
It surely won't take long.
I'll just bide my time
And everything will be fine.
          Stuck in time……doing nothing.

ELEVEN MONTHS AGO

These months, following the death of my sweetheart dear,
Have not been easy for me to endure.
But days have been spent and months have gone by,
And somehow now it's less that I cry.

I've struggled through papers and very odd forms.
I've filled in dates....like when we were born.
Even the one that said we were wed,
In order to prove that I was not dead.

I managed to shop and even enjoy
Preparing for birthdays of each girl and boy.
I really took pride telling folks in the store
Of fourteen grandchildren and the births of three more.

Now shopping for Christmas is so hard to do,
Especially when it's always been done by two.
I've tried to do it this year with a new attitude,
One of thanksgiving and even of gratitude.

Because celebrating the birth of Jesus
Has always been very important to us.
I will prepare a card with my thoughts in verse
And hope that we all can appreciate His birth.

A birth is something to reassure as rare,
That we only have one is fair.
But fairer still...a gift to each one
Comes to us from God in the birth of His Son.

continued

And so in thanksgiving and gratitude to Him,
I'll shop for gifts and send cards to a friend.
I'll celebrate THE GIFT that He has given
And rejoice that my loved one, through faith, is in heaven.

I pray that you do understand THAT birth
And what it means to us here on earth.
I pray that His gift of life and not loss
Is real, as you look beyond to the cross.

STAYING BUSY

Our anniversary is usually near Easter. So, I try to attend an out of town Easter presentation and stay with friends, or at a motel. Also, during the Christmas holidays, I try to go out of town at least once for a different view.

His birthday is near the date of his death date, so I try to plan a busy week with people or meetings that hold my attention.

I try to surround myself on "difficult days" with people and places I know and love, and with tasks that bring me varied pleasures or rewards.

I try to do things that don't require couples. But, I definitely stay involved in the world. It would have been easy to cocoon …In fact, for the first six months, I did do exactly that. A dear friend came one day and lovingly, and persistently, waited until I got bathed, dressed and ready to go to lunch with her. That was when GOD spoke to me and told me that He took David…not me, and that there was still work for me to do.

I needed to begin building my own memories. Usually when I speak to groups, I refer to things that are current in my life……………now I have some things I can use for illustrations and not continue being a tear-jerking speaker, as I have been for the past two years.

Writing my separate book of grief poems has been helpful—-but I didn't share them with anyone as openly as my regular poems. Finally, I am beginning to merge some of those poems into appropriate speeches. It has been good therapy. Journaling has been a good discipline for me. I'd rather write poetry, but I see the value of journaling. It is different from writing a speech and I really have to work at it.

One of my daughters-in-law (Marsha Allison Christian) wrote these words on what would have been David's birthday (February 3), as she was going through her journey of grief after David's passing:

continued

Granddaddy

Granddaddy loved the babies.
They were dearest to his heart.
When he held one in his arms,
You couldn't pry them apart.

He'd meet us at the door,
With arms opened wide
And say, "Granddaddy wants the baby"
Before we ever got inside.

But there was one of his babies
That he couldn't hold and love.
For this baby was with Jesus,
And waiting up above.

Waiting for his Granddaddy
To join him in Glory.
To sit upon his grandad's lap
And hear him read a story.

"Granddaddy, I've been waiting here
Patiently for you—-
I'm glad you're finally here with me—
We have so much to do.

"We can travel on the streets of gold,
Take a long and happy hike
Or weave between the clouds—us two
On your heavenly motorbike."

These babies here will miss him,
But he's as busy as can be.
Doing what he loved the very most…
For all eternity!

DROP OUT

After David died, it would have been easy
    For me to drop out................
        Of my circle of friends
        Of my involvement in civic groups
        Of my leadership places
        Of my role as mom and grandmother
        Of my.....................

My eyes were heavy with tears.
I was tired from lack of sleep.
I was physically tired and emotionally exhausted,
But spiritually, I felt close to God.

I thought about His grace and mercy
That I'd experienced personally,
Before and after David's death.
That's what kept me going on the journey.

TEARS OF LOVE

Thirty-six years so full of love,
Given and blessed by God above,
Were not wasted on the young,
But freely given to all around.

Now, when grief crowds in on me,
I look around and always see
Extensions of those loving years.
And then I wipe away my tears.

Now I see our love expressed,
For in our children we were blessed.
Blessed in their choices for a spouse,
As with children they fill their house.

Blessed by God with children...in reality
Born to us, both physically and spiritually.
Born to be nurtured every day,
Born to be guided to follow His way.

So while I deeply miss my sweetheart,
I really am very, very thankful
That for thirty-six years He let us be a part
Of seeing what we really live for.

MY CHOICE

I choose not to focus on the loss of David. I choose, rather, to celebrate the memories and to work toward some of the goals we'd set together. I choose to function as a person who is alive, and who has something to contribute to society. I know there will be many more times of pain in my future, but that's life. That's what makes giving HOPE to people worth doing. To grow through and beyond the pain of this life, knowing this life is really temporary. Then, someday, we'll go beyond pain as we know it and sit at God's feet, as brother and sister worshiping The One who deserves all worship and praise!

STEPS IN TIME

As we leave steps along the shore,
They remind us of His steps in days of yore.
Days when His step meant He'd come to bring
The message allowing the sorrowing to sing.

He gave the message that all might see
The steps that lead to eternity.
Eternity begins at the path on the shore,
With destination settled before we reach death's door.

What will others think of our steps in time?
Will they see the message in each line?
Will they choose to follow along The Way,
So we'll arrive together on Judgment Day?

SINCE I'M GOING ANYWAY

    I must be willing to change my schedule. Such as in: Evangelism…be willing to witness and challenge others to know Him, or to learn more about His will for their lives. If my schedule doesn't place me with those to whom I would feel comfortable giving a witness, I must listen seriously to their story and then encourage them to find options of how to deal with their situation.

    I must be ready for Him to open my eyes and to enlarge my vision… even if it means a change of address. That's what happened (sort of). He guided me to take the CPE (Clinical Pastoral Education) training for a year in a town two hours away. He provided a stranger to give me a key to her house, with full confidence and encouragement that during one of my speeches, God had told her to do that.

    Do I need to change anything else in my lifestyle to be more effective in witnessing? Such as in: my home, my church, my business dealings, my community involvement, my world, my leisure……?

    In Southern Slang, could part of Matthew 28:19-20 read: "…being as how you're going anyway, do this?"

Do I have a marketplace style evangelism?
Where am I the most phony?
Where am I the most comfortable?
Where does God seem closest?
What do I want God to do…
                For me?
                In me?
                With me?
                Through me?
                To me?

    I'd better plan more quiet time, more time to read and, of course, more time to write.

                                                        continued

I really did plan to read and write the hour it was expected to have my car serviced, but there were people who just needed to talk (one at a time). I soon learned why I was there at that specific time, and that the car was just a reason to be where He wanted me to be. Each person was at a different level from the others, but each had real needs, real questions, and each was open to talking about Him. One of those persons developed into a prayer partner for me. Praise God!

READY OR NOT

As members of the human race, we knew we would die someday.

As children of God, we knew human death was but "a crossing" or "a changing".

When we were confronted with the reality of a failing heart, we knew each day was a gift.

We were thankful for each day, for each medical procedure, for each breakthrough in medicine.

But, we were not ready to give up and face the facts that death brings. Perhaps he was ready-since he had experienced the pain of a failing heart- but I certainly was not. I clung to each day and was thankful for it. When the phone call came, I was not ready for it. He'd gone "running" that morning, before getting ready for church, and died before he hit the ground. That's how the doctor described what happened when David's heart stopped beating. There was a paramedic and an ambulance at the corner when he fell, and they did all they could do. I knew—-but I was not ready.

   Not ready for being alone,
   Not ready for missing him,
   Not ready for changing goals,
   Not ready for changing lifestyle.

I am thankful that God has been with us through all of our marriage journey.

   He gave us each other.
   He gave us five wonderful children.
   He gave us wonderful spouses for the children.
   He gave us seventeen special grandchildren.
   He gave us wonderful groups of friends (most of whom are fellow believers).

continued

But, most of all, I thank God for the HOPE that we have…that as we give up our human bodies here, we are but a blink away from our spiritual bodies and eternity with Him. That, one day, I will again be with David—not as his beloved wife—but as his sister, sitting with him at the feet of our merciful Father.

A CHRISTMAS MOURNING

Another wonderful Christmas season has just come and gone. We had worshiped in our church sanctuary with family and friends, rejoicing over the event of our Savior's birth. We had no idea that only four weeks later, we would again gather in that same sanctuary with family and friends, in another service honoring the life of my husband—the father of our five children.

He had been a part of the presentation of The Lord's Supper Service only a month ago, and now he was feasting at The Lord's table.

His brother, sister and their extended families had been here to joyfully celebrate another family reunion just three weeks ago…and now were here to celebrate and mourn his passing.

That Sunday morning, as I awaited his return from his morning jogging time, I had no idea that he was already at the hospital and that he'd already "passed on". As the nurse was calling me, our doctor was calling his church about the passing of one of their friends. After I received the call, I called our church and each of our children who, in turn, called their in-laws and then each called their churches. That fatal morning, ten churches were praying for our family and three of them were televised. God was announcing to the world that He had taken another faithful warrior home.

We are grateful for our church families, standing and kneeling with us, as they mourned with us.

The next Christmas was especially difficult for me until, again, realized that The Birth we celebrate allows death's sting to be only an earthly pain that is temporary. Easter came…..He arose!

My focus then changed to the joy of an eternity to be together. Eternity to worship and praise Him whose family we are.

DEATH'S STING

Right now, I feel a deep, deep sting
And I cannot in victory sing.
For the death of one so dear
Brings real earthly pain so clear.

So I'll cling to His Word,
And the Holy promises I've heard.
I'll remember past times,
Filled with blessings divine.

One day I will sing again,
As time seems to ease my pain.
I'll rejoice that my loved one
Has the eternal promise to claim.

Death's sting, as I see clearer,
Has only a temporary hold that's nearer.
But as time turns into eternity,
Death's sting has no reality.

THE SHOWER BRUSH

I stepped into the shower and found in there
His shampoo brush, all matted with hair.
Those hairs of red and grey-like silver
Became something I could now treasure.

I don't think others would understand
The value I place on each hair strand.
But save them I will and someday then,
I'll have a remembrance of my dear friend.

CRYING

It's been one month now since David died,
A month of days through which I've cried.
Four long weeks have gone so slow
And left me wondering how to go.

How will go on, I cry.
Why did my sweetheart have to die?
Why not me, so he could live?
My tears pour out as from a sieve.

How I long to share these days
With one who understands the ways?
I've tried to express His love to me
And tell how I've felt His victory.

Friends say that I did good
And they encourage me as they should.
But still I feel so incomplete.
To me, these days are not sweet.

I long to hear the words so true.
Words to correct the things I do.
I long to be understood and rated.
I long for—————————-David.

HOVERING

As a bride, I learned to know his love was real.
I did not need "that touch" to feel.
So I learned there was no need to hover,
To give ourselves room lest we smother.

As I stood at the bedside, when he was ill,
I knew even then his love was real.
So I learned again there was no need to hover,
To give ourselves room lest we smother.

As I stand at the gravesite after his death,
I knew that true love has a greater depth.
So I learned again there was no need to hover,
To give myself room lest I smother.

AT THE CEMETARY

So many flowers across the hillside.
So many loved ones on the other side.
So many memories,
So many dreams,
So many plans,
So many schemes,
So many tears shed at this place.
So many petitions to the Father for grace.

SEASONS

I have learned in my life that God gives me seasons of time to be in certain circumstances, or with particular people at certain places, or series of places for specific times of need in my own life. Sometimes it's been my need for inspiration, encouragement, healing, ministry or several other specific needs in my personal journey.

One of the hardest lessons for me to learn has been to know when one season ends and another begins.

An illustration of that is related to my singing. I don't sing, well, not so as anyone would want to hear. After I'd been in the grief process, following David's death, God thrust me into three Senior Adult choir groups. In fact, I usually am discouraged from singing out loud when near good singers. But God knew that I needed the discipline of learning new arrangements to the old songs and to learn some new ones. I really needed the fellowship and affirmation that I received from those special seniors—the role models, the encouragement, the inspiration, the wonderful way they made me feel needed, even the acknowledgment that I could still minister to others and meet some of their needs.

All of a sudden, I could follow the director, I could follow printed music and I knew what those signs meant on the notes. Boy! I was even able to help someone else. I was doing great—well, I was mouthing it less and less, and I was singing out and loving it.

Then God said, "There's something else I want you to do now." I said, "But, Lord, I like this—this is great. Thank You for the gift." He said, "It is preparation for something—get ready to move on." "But, Lord, I still need this right now."

In order to get me to where He could move me, He removed the joy from my heart. I could still sing and be with those choirs, but the circumstances were now difficult. I still loved everyone and yet, I knew that I shouldn't be there.

I still maintain a great fellowship with those people and some are my dearest friends. But, I no longer set my schedule around those circumstances. God is walking me into another season of my life, and I'm looking forward to finding out just what part music will play in that future season.

Now, it's four months later, and two of those choirs presented concert selections at our wedding. Yes, God brought love into my old life and heart again.

I rejoice to say that God still has a plan for my life, and I want to praise Him as I move into another season. I wonder what that new song is that He is giving me.

Truly, God's plan for Loyd and me to marry, and for me to be appointed a missionary to Brazil was a total surprise to me. The sweet story of our time together is beautiful and for another time to share. The fact that we soon were deep into his journey of Alzheimer's Disease is difficult for me to recount.

As newlyweds, we went to Brazil for him to "show-off" his new bride to his friends and students, in the place he'd spent almost fifty years of his life. He and Mary Hazel (his first wife) had been appointed, served and retired, but continued to serve as volunteers until her death— one month after David's death.

At first, I explained away "little" things he began doing, after a few years of marriage. I said it was just settling into another lifestyle after being single for four years. When time came that I knew I couldn't speak well enough to communicate with the medical community, I knew it was time to return to the states.

I'm sure the grief he felt as he knew something was wrong, but couldn't do anything about it, must have been severe. He'd always been able to adapt to changes and different lifestyles. He was an Old Testament scholar and a great Bible teacher. The grief I felt, as I saw our world changing and nothing could be done about it, was extreme. How could I adjust to taking care of a man who wasn't the man that I married just a few years ago?

I treasure a poem, which he wrote for me in the months of our courtship:

I often think of you on wakeful nights,
When the wind blows softly through the leaves.
Through my open window, the late lights
Rock drowsily in the gentle southern breeze.
Yet standing here alone, I can but pray
This gentle breeze could swiftly blow your way,
Whispering the words of love I long so much to say.

HOW DO I LOVE A MAN WHO ISN'T THE MAN I MARRIED?

In desperation, I prayed, "Lord, what happened...this isn't how it's supposed to be. This isn't what I thought was going to happen. What's going on? True, I did say that I wanted to do Your will, that I wanted to honor You in my life, that I *wanted to be guided by You. But, Lord, this? We made all these plans of how we would spend our senior days. This wasn't in those plans."*

True, this wasn't in our plans, but I know God is always faithful and that He will get me through the future unknown. The Lord knows I need lots of details, encouragement and information to do anything. So, of course, He blessed me with more training, courses and caring people to walk with us through these difficult days and years.

Any amount of change was hard for me. At my age, this extreme change was challenging. It was hard to cope with the changes that were happening in Loyd and not being able to talk with him about it.

I am thankful that I had caring friends and leaders, in addition to the conference speakers who had great knowledge on the subject. I kept praying that God would continue to guide me and, at the same time, that He would work on my attitude. After He gave me Ecclesiastes 5:20, I was able to relax my worries about Loyd's status. Then He gave me Phil 3:13-14, to help me relax my anxieties about our plans and goals. Having support groups to attend was a great help for me. There, no one would think bad of you for expressing your true feelings about what was happening or about fears of the "what if's".

THE COINS

I've been on the verge of tears all day, since my good cry early this morning. This morning, during our domino game, Loyd pulled from his pocket a handful of coins and looked at one of them. He showed it to me and said, "This isn't any good anymore, is it?" I'm sure he was remembering the changing of currency so often in Brazil. I said, "Yes, it's a nickel." He then placed the four dimes and two pennies in a row by the nickel. After what seemed to me like hours, he pushed them forward and said, "You will have to count them, my glasses aren't doing so good." I said, "You have forty seven cents." He then pulled out the bills and said, "One, two, three...that makes forty-seven and three makes fifty dollars." "Excuse me," I said, "you have enough to do whatever you want to do." He said, "When we go to lunch, I want to get a paper." I try to be reassuring to him, even though I would rather cry some more.

His Fear

Sometimes, I had a sitter come to play dominoes with him or to watch a replay of a baseball game. On one such occasion, when I returned, she had a note for me:

Judi; He has been extremely in fear of your placing him into a facility today. This began about 10 am and continued all day...he thinks you are making those arrangements now. He asked Tina (our housekeeper) and me to pray for him that he would be able to stay at home. He asked me to stay until you got home and to talk you out of that notion.

Progression

My brother, Jerry, said, "You know that you love a person when you can clean up the bathroom mess and not feel like scolding them good." Yes, now, I know what he meant.

He is so child-like but, as an adult, he is worthy of all the respect and dignity I can give him. My love for him is so different now from what it was when we married. I don't want to pity him, but I am sad for such an intelligent man having to go through this. My love for him compels me to assist him all that I can.

He gets so little exercise that I often go with him to the mailbox every hour, just to get in a walk.

One day, he asked me where I lived. He has memorized his wife's name, but doesn't know that I am her. When I told him my name was Judi, he was surprised. He said his Judi would be back in a few minutes and that I would like her.

Loyd seemed to be seriously considering something in his mind. He finally said, "Of all the girls I live with, you are the one I love." He was confusing his sitters with living here.

I think one of my highest points of grief for Loyd was when I had to place him into a facility. At that point, he was not aware of where he was nor of who people were.

THE ILLNESS

I'm so sad I can hardly write.
His illness is one we cannot fight.
The meds slowed the progress for a while,
But now there's little room for a smile.

Pain is not a problem with which we deal,
And he really does enjoy each little meal.
Cookies and ice cream an extra measure
Go a long way toward giving him pleasure.

Visits with friends bring special joy.
He gets excited like a little boy.
Although after a while, he's forgotten their name.
We know he's happy all the same.

Alzheimer's Disease, the mysterious plight,
Has brought to us days dark as night.
It seemed to come so unexpected.
The whole family has been affected.

Highly educated, he knew so much.
And yet with people, he's not lost touch.
An Old Testament scholar, a teacher of The Word,
A professor to those who wanted to learn.

The president of a seminary in a distant land,
He spoke a language we didn't understand.
He groomed and trained young men and women
To serve in positions to which they seemed driven.

As he lost touch with our reality,
He seemed to have a joy and delight daily.
His peace in confusion caused us to question
Could this disease be to him a blessing?

Though he is different, we love him still
And pray that someday medicine will
Help others be saved from this strange illness
That robs the mind, though it's been quite blessed.

My sadness remains, and yet I am joyful
To have known a man that was so truthful.
He influenced so many before me
And now he's gone on to his eternity.

OVERWHELMED

My mind is disturbed.
My heart is torn.
My hands tremble.
My knees fail me.
My eyes gush with tears.
My mouth roars in pain.
My lungs groan in despair.
Taste is null to my tongue.

No compassion comes from friends.
I am distraught.
I am destroyed.
I am blown by the wind.
I chase the wind.
I am as a child, who
Resisting being born needs a
Refreshing push or a
Beautiful flower needs care
And fragrance to be complete.

A Song

Today, alone, I must continue on.
True love has given me a song.
A song expressed in the love I share,
By acts to others that show I care.

THE PEACE

Where life abides, peace can come
But grace must be the first one.
Only then can peace be true.
That's the way it'll work for you.

When we accept God's grace for us,
We reap the peace of The Cross.
We can approach His throne as we are
And see our sins banished afar.

HOW LONG

My heart aches for the one I miss.
While I grieve, I cannot feel bliss.
How long will I be like this?
How long will I taste his kiss?

MY HEART AND BONES

I read about being alive
And knowing that He lives.
I know in my heart that He reigns
And that for me He is.
But yet I feel overcome and alone.
I feel a sadness in each bone.

SPELL IT OUT

What do I fear—?
Surely not the unknown,
For He walks with me.
I am not alone.
So what do I fear—?

What makes me feel afraid?
I want to spell It out clear,
So at His feet it can be laid.
When will life return to me,
To bring me back to reality?
When will I again be free,
To love and laugh and just be me?

I WILL

So much needs to be done,
So many claims on my life.
Yet unashamedly I say,
I will serve Him who saved me.

Some want me to assist their cause.
Some want me to tout their claim.
Lest I be caught up with much to do,
I will serve Him who saved me.

My personal needs are strained.
My mental needs are strong.
My spiritual needs are great.
I will serve Him who saved me.

My pride and ego rise in my mind.
They call attention to my – great value,
But this I know—He values me.
So I will serve Him who saved me.

I WISH

I wish that my mind was clear,
To relive memories that could cheer.
I wish to escape the reality
Of what this death really means to me.

REMEMBERING

Your generous smile,
A wonderful treat,
Still causes my heart
To skip a beat.

This ring on my finger,
This love in my heart
Keeps my life happy,
Though we are apart.

NOW

I must be busy, I must prepare.
I must be alert for time to share,
To share a love that He has given
And let them know how to be forgiven.
And now I know this is the time
To share His love with friends of mine.
Friends who think there's time to wait,
Before thinking long about their fate.
Time gets away from us so fast.
This is the time to release our past.
Release those burdens at His feet
And then experience victory, sweet
Victory, over sins that bind us.
To the one always behind us,
To the one who always tries
To make us swallow all his lies.
Life here is so temporary
That there isn't time to tarry.
Trust in Christ as Lord today
And He will wipe your sins away.

DIFFERENCE

*These rings on my right hand
Seem so out of place,
As does this furrow in my brow
That's growing on my face.*

*Life for me really has taken on
A different pace,
As I consider paths to take
While continuing to run the race.*

THE CHANGING DISEASE

I do not like the way I feel.
I'd like to pretend it is not real.
But real it is, I must admit,
And somehow now I'll manage it.

This feeling of anger must be faced
With all it's timing to be traced.
So that we see its root so clear
Is opposite all that I hold dear.

I'm angry that I acted bad
In making choices that I had.
I'll try next time to think it through
And factor in a love that's true.

My love for him must change direction.
To be this way was not his intention.
His brain has changed, no one is to blame.
Alzheimer's Disease means we will change.

He is changing, regardless of his will.
I must change because I will.
I will treat him with loving respect,
With every day that we have left.

FIRST TIME OUT

Her purse on her shoulder.
The keys in her hand
Made her feel bolder,
As she climbed in the van.

This day, she felt good.
Her mom said, "OK".
Her dad said she could
Drive friends home today.

Then on the road,
Approaching the light,
Was a man who was old,
Not walking just right.

Her friends said, "don't stop,
Let someone else help him".
But her heart reached out,
As though he were kin.

With cheer in her throat,
And sounding quite cool,
She said she'd get him help
If he wanted her to.

He said "yes, God bless you",
Gave her a number to call,
As he took another step-then two,
Looking like he would fall.

Next day a visit from a daughter
Brought thank you and tears
For helping her father,
A patient with Alzheimer's.

IT'S NOT HER

*I want to cry, but there is no time.
I want to scream, but how would that seem?
Why can't I adjust, why can't I cope?
Why do I feel there is no hope?*

*I didn't choose this, I ask, why me?
The timing's not right. this should not be.
She was so smart, she was so alert.
She knew just how to sooth each hurt.*

*Now her mind is so mixed-up.
She calls this pen her coffee cup.
How can I stand to see her this way?
How can I help, what can I say?*

*I loved her so much, the one that she was.
How can I like the one that she is?
And yet I will find a way,
To help this one on this new day.*

*I will because of what she means to me.
To all those memories in all our dreams,
The one who is———yet
Isn't really her.*

THINKING THOUGHTS

As I think of loved ones departed,
Here I sit, all broken hearted.
Those who once gave good advice
Are now thoughts that still are nice.

As I contemplate memories dear,
I consider when my time is near.
Will their thoughts be those of love
And that my spirit abides above?

How will others' remembrances be
When their thoughts might turn to me?
Will there be happy thoughts to cheer,
Or moments of quiet and maybe a tear?
Whatever thoughts that then may be,
I'll continue to just be me
And live each day to stay on track.
I'll not live by looking back.

SO MUST I

Now sitting here alone, after burying a dad and two husbands, I am physically alone, but I do not feel alone.

I know that just as my name, Moon, has a meaning, my life has meaning. As the moon has no life nor light of itself, so have I no light nor life of myself. As the moon is only a blessing to those on earth, as it reflects the light of the sun—

So must I....

So, today, I realize God's meaning and call on my life is to simply be a reflection of His Son's light to those on this earth while I am here. I don't need to preach or expound on His word. I only need to share with people His word in me. As I continue my "read the Bible Through", I pray that His words will become such a part of my life that people will see Him as events unfold around me.

Alone, I am of no value——My only importance comes as I reflect Him to others. So must I...

WAIT? UNTIL I'M HOW OLD?

I knew beyond a shadow of a doubt that I was going to a "far away land" to "do missions". I had felt that call on my life as a pre-teen. Then, while in college, I knew that I was to marry David. But his call was to be a full-time christian, while being an engineer in the USA. We birthed and raised each of our five children to be completely sold-out to Christ and missions. We even raised a niece and a nephew. But, still, not one person had been called to a "far away land".

After some "in the country" mission trips, and the death of my husband of thirty-six years, I questioned my understanding of God's call on my life. Three years later, God had me and my new husband of six months appointed ISC (International Service Corps Missionaries) to a "far away land". I was sixty years old! It reminded me of Abraham and Sara. I then realized that I'd spent most of my life preparing for that experience. Also, within four years of that time, my eldest daughter and her husband, after having six children, were called to another "far away land". Truly, God works in mysterious ways.

I finally realized that God equips us for what He wants us to do and He prepares us for when He wants us to do the "event". We need to simply be obedient, learn from each encounter, or experience, and wait upon His leadership.

WHAT'S IN A NAME

When I was Judi Jacobson, my dad used to say, "Remember whose you are and don't disgrace our name." These words had an impact on my life!

When I was Judi Christian, I realized again the reality of my dad's words, and took the application further to hear my heavenly Father say, "Remember whose you are and don't disgrace our name."

When I was Judi Moon, I again saw beyond the physical union of a man and woman, and heard our Father again say, "remember whose you are and don't disgrace our name."

I have a family—a big one, which includes the Jacobsons, the Christians and the Moons, which brings to us all the blessings, limitations and frailties of human beings. My heritage and lineage is long and full of events that show our humanity, and point to our need of That One who alone can bring forgiveness and salvation with the promise of eternal life.

My prayer now is that you know Him and have peace in your life.... regardless of the situations on your journey.

Judith Elaine Jacobson Christian Moon

DEATH AND THE SURVIVOR

I. Death happens
    A. It is a part of life.
    B. It is no respecter of persons, age, education, economics, influence, health, environment, personality, nor of any bargaining tool.
    C. There is no way to undo it.
       Not bargaining, anger, shock nor denial.

II. Life goes on for the survivors
    A. The survivor must be allowed to seek out all avenues of possibilities to "undo" the death and the unfairness of it.
    B. The emotional "good-bye" or the "letting go" of the deceased must be on the survivor's own terms, as he/she encounters his own humanity and relationship to God.
    C. Only by fully realizing the loss can the survivor "live" again—emotionally,
            Physically,
            Intellectually,
            Spiritually,
            Socially.

III. The survivor has needs
    A. Understanding
       The loss is shocking and painful.
       It disrupts all plans and goals.
       It changes the focus of the survivor.
       It changes the personality of the survivor.
    B. Patience
       Adjusting to the loss is not easy.
       Refocusing goals takes time.
       Stages of grief must be rehashed,
       many times for some survivors.
       Emotions are on the surface and erupt at odd times.
       Survivors are strangers to themselves.
       There seems to be no place for them.

1. Couple's groups are now awkward.
2. Single's groups are focused on different goals than the new survivor is currently.

The survivor's self-worth is at stake—anger, envy, jealousy and resentment can take over for a while. "Cocooning" can happen too quickly, unless a friend carefully steps in to assist.

C. Acceptance
...Allow the survivor to be in grief,
Thoughts for them are short and fragmented.
Realize that those emotions are temporary,
That they are impatient with where they are in the grief process.
That they are judgmental of themselves,
That they are frustrated over their lack of control,
That they are seeking to find their new identity,
That they fear they're "going crazy".
Allow the survivor to talk about the deceased
Or, not to talk, if that is their choice.
Don't rush them to "get on with life".
Allow them "down times" to be sad.
Encourage development of the survivor's positive,
    Talents and abilities at a slow pace.
Allow for relapses.
Just "be there"—silences are OK.
Don't try to give advice,
    To explain away the pain,
    To offer security,
    To be condescending,
Do be honest.
    Be positive.
    Be tactful.
Offer or help them to see alternatives.
Remind them of HOPE in faith.
Grieve in your own way—on another level.

continued

Respect the survivor's faith level.

IV. Therefore, the survivor needs someone who will
   A. Offer HOPE
       Hope that time and work lessen pain.
       That there is a future for them,
       That memories influence forever.
   B. Believe in their self-worth
       That they have value,
       That they can refocus,
       That they are needed.
   C. To be honest with them,
       To all that happens,
       To recognize past as influence,
       To see now as a reality.
   D. Give them permission to grieve.
   E. Be at peace with their own mortality.
   F. Be at peace with their own faith.
   G. Realize that there are some areas of life over which we have no control.
   H. Offer HOPE as a foundation for growing personally as an individual.

There is no problem in seeking professional help. Many doctors are willing to assist the survivor in working out some details. Also, professional counselors are usually quite good at their job. Sometimes a pharmacist can help organize the medicine schedule. There are support groups available and may be of value to you. Usually, what is needed most is patience and time, with respect to personal needs and preferences.

I really appreciate having friends that will pray for me, even if I don't get specific about the request. Anyone who wants to know all the details is just being too nosey. (My elderly friend, years ago, used to call those folks "busybodies".)

Most of all, be confident of the fact that God knows and understands. Know that He is on your side and wants the best for you. I pray that the Holy Spirit guide you, as you progress on your journey.

About the Author

*B*orn *in Minneapolis, Minnesota, Judi has been a resident of Madison County, Alabama since 1960 and a resident of Alabama for over 60 years. Judi has been widowed twice. She is mother to two sons, three daughters and three step-sons...all of whom are married and have given Judi twenty-eight grandchildren. Twelve of those grands are married and have given her twelve great-grandchildren.*

Judi is involved in mission activities locally, statewide, nationally and internationally. She is a member of many clubs and agencies, locally, statewide, nationally and internationally. Judi works with the National Alliance for Mental Illness and is a Family to Family teacher, along with the NAMI class to professionals. She teaches Internationals English as a Second Language and also teaches Adults Reading and Writing. She is a source of support to caregivers of Alzheimer's patients in support of the Alzheimer's Association.

In her spare time, Judi loves to read, write poetry, speak to groups about many issues and go on mission trips (she has been to twenty-three countries and forty-five states). Judi's involvement with the mentally ill of her community and state means that she is on call 24-7, and that helps her in reaching her goals.

She uses her poetry and life experiences to entertain, inspire and motivate others. She wishes to be encouraged, inspired and enriched, and she wishes to encourage, inspire and enrich others. She chooses to be physically alert and assist physically in sharing a vision with those who have no vision.

THE END

"That's all folks"

Means this is the end,

But we'll meet again,
My friend.

For wheels are rolling,

And words are surging.

As one thought is folding,

And another emerging.

www.ingramcontent.com/pod-product-compliance
Ingram Content Group UK Ltd.
Pitfield, Milton Keynes, MK11 3LW, UK
UKHW022220230426
12048UKWH00016BA/956